THE WESTERN YORKSHIRE DALES

Keith Wood

First published in Great Britain in 2011

British Library Cataloguing-in-Publication Data
A CIP record for this title is available from the British Library

ISBN 978 0 85710 040 5

PiXZ Books
Halsgrove House, Ryelands Business Park,
Bagley Road, Wellington, Somerset TA21 9PZ
Tel: 01823 653777
Fax: 01823 216796
email: sales@halsgrove.com

An imprint of Halstar Ltd, part of the Halsgrove group of companies
Information on all Halsgrove titles is available at: www.halsgrove.com

Printed and bound in China by Toppan Leefung Printing Ltd

Contents

How to use this book

The Western Dales consist of a number of separate valleys on the western fringes of the Yorkshire Dales National Park. These include: Malhamdale, Ribblesdale, Crummackdale, Clapdale, Thornton Dale, Kingsdale and Dentdale; all of which are visited in one way or another in this collection of walks. Most of the walks are easily accessed from the A65 trunk road running between the market towns of Skipton and Kirkby Lonsdale.

Geographically this is limestone country and the impact of the glaciers and subsequent melt waters from the last Ice Age can be seen across the area, leaving the most spectacular limestone architecture in the country; magnificent dry coves such as Malham Cove, Goredale Scar and Trow Gill; limestone cliffs, including Smearsett Scar, Attermire Scar and Twisleton Scar; and vast areas of limestone pavement above Malham Cove and Twisleton Scars.

The Western Dales also includes the area known as the Three Peaks comprising Pen-y-ghent, Ingleborough and the highest, Whernside. These three mountains dominate the views across the district and in fact the distinctive shape of Ingleborough is visible from at least six of the ten walks, and therefore I have included the ascent of Ingleborough as one of the routes.

All of these features combine to make this a popular walking district evidenced by the fact that three long distance trails pass through the area: the Pennine Way, the Ribble Way and the Dales Way; sections of all three are used in the walks.

Each route is graded from Easy to More Challenging with further details of distance, height ascended and the type of terrain covered, to help with decisions of which walk to choose. The information blocks have distances and height gained in both imperial and metric measures, whereas in the body of the text I have kept to the old imperial units which still feel more appropriate (and comfortable) when describing the walks.

The walks are covered by the Ordnance Survey Explorer Maps OL:2 Yorkshire Dales Western Area and OL: 10 Yorkshire Dales Southern Area. The maps in this book are only an outline version of each walk and the detail provided by the OS maps puts each route in context.

Every year tens of thousands of visitors enjoy the dales with the vast majority coming to no harm. However there are many cases each year where walkers are injured, get lost or find themselves in some other kind difficulty requiring the assistance of the Rescue Services. A few simple precautions should help avoid any problems:

- If you are unsure about your fitness start with the walks graded Easy and work your way up to More Challenging.
- Wear suitable footwear- properly fitted walking boots are recommended for all the walks.
- Take suitable clothing; the weather in the Yorkshire Dales can change very quickly, take a waterproof and extra warm layers to wear.
- Take plenty to eat and drink en route, dehydration and lack of nourishment can lead to fatigue and mistakes being made.
- An outline map illustrates each walk but it is recommended that a complete detailed 1:25000 map is taken.
- Inform someone of your planned route and expected return time.
- Check the weather forecast in advance and only take to the more challenging routes on clear days.
- And finally keep to the paths and watch where you are putting your feet - most accidents are caused by careless slips!

Useful websites:

Yorkshire Dales National Park
www.yorkshiredales.org.uk

Yorkshire Dales Society
www.yds.org.uk

Yorkshire Dales Millennium Trust
www.ydmt.org

Out of Oblivion Yorkshire Dales Heritage and Archaeology
www.outofoblivion.org.uk

Yorkshire Dales Tourism
www.yorkshiredalesandharrogate.com

Traveldales – Public Transport Information
www.traveldales.org.uk

Keith Wood Photography
www.keithwoodphotography.co.uk

Key to Symbols Used

Level of difficulty:

Easy ♥

Fair ♥ ♥

More challenging ♥ ♥ ♥

Map symbols:

- Park & start
- Tarred Road
- ----- Footpath
- ■ Building / Town
- Pub
- ▲ Landmark
- ||||||| Railway
- —— River

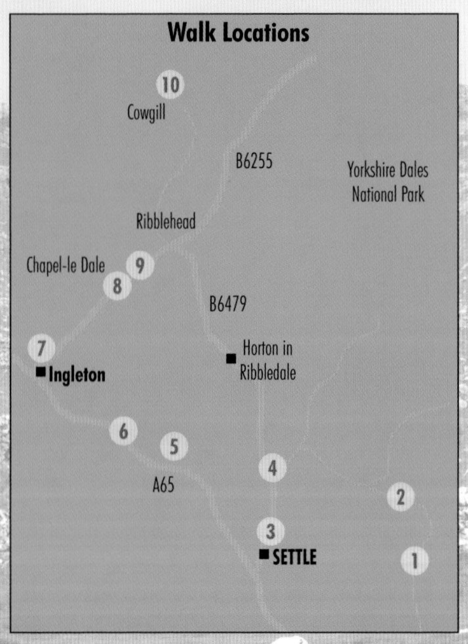

1 Malham Cove and Goredale Scar

Start by visiting one of Yorkshire iconic locations

This "Malham Spectacular" makes the ideal introduction to this collection of walks in the magnificent limestone scenery of the Western Dales. Malham Cove is a huge natural amphitheatre of limestone which rises over 200 feet (70m) above the valley floor topped by one of the best sections of limestone pavement in the country. The walk leads to the adjacent valley with the equally spectacular Goredale Scar. Both are remnants from the last Ice Age when huge waterfalls of melt water would have flowed over the tops of both cliffs. The walk visits the much smaller and secluded Janet's Foss falls on the return leg.

Goredale Scar
Goredale Beck
Janet's Foss
Malham Beck
Malham
Mires Barn

Looking along Malham Beck to Malham Cove

Level:
Length: 4.5 miles (7.2km)
Ascent: 600 feet (180m)
Terrain: Clear paths throughout with steep climb up steps to the top of Malham Cove
Park and Start: YDNP car park at Malham GR 900 627
Info: Toilets at start, various refreshment opportunities in Malham
www.malhamdale.com

1 Park in the YDNP car park at the edge of Malham village. Leaving the car park turn left to walk along the road through the village. Pass The Buck Inn and the village store and continue to walk along the quiet road out of the top of the village, following the crowds on a busy day to the spectacle of Malham Cove. Leave the road at Town Head Farm and take the well laid path through the gate on the right sign-posted "Malham Cove ½ mile". The path follows the route of the Pennine Way and before long the magnificent spectacle of the dry limestone cliffs of Malham Cove comes into view. Follow the well laid path to the foot of the cove beside Malham Beck.

Malham Cove

The Buck Inn, Malham

2 Approaching the base of the cove the path forks; take the path on the left to climb the stepped path up the left hand side of the cove. Pausing to catch your breath as height is gained there are ever improving views back along to Malham. Reaching the top you arrive at the impressive limestone pavement above the cove with its clints and grikes; swing around to the right following one of the many paths around the top of the cove. Just watch every step you take on the potentially ankle breaking limestone pavement, taking care not to damage this precious landscape.

3 At the far end of the cove a drystone wall is reached with the sign "Footpath Goredale 1¼ miles". Follow the clear path on short cropped turf on this popular route heading towards Goredale. The path makes its way on the level around Sheriff Hill with limestone formations all around and views across Malham Dale to Kirkby Fell. Climb the ladder

The area above the cove is known as limestone pavement. It is made up of large blocks of limestone which are known as clints separated by deep cracks or fissures called grikes. Many rare wild flowers make their home on the protected limestone pavement.

Looking along Malham Beck to Malham Cove

stile into Malham Rakes lane; cross straight over the lane following the finger post "FP Goredale ¾ mile". Follow the clear stony path through the pastures above Cordon Flats Barn along to Goredale. Follow the gravel path above the intake wall on the way to Goredale with views to the right onto the village of Malham. The path drops down round a subsidiary dry valley. Follow the fingerpost sign to Goredale through a walkers' gate on the right through the wall and take the green path down through the pastures to meet the road at Goredale Bridge.

4 The path emerges onto the road at Goredale Bridge. Turn left and walk along the road for 50 yards and take the gate on the left signed "FP Goredale Scar ½ mile" along the gravel path with the magnificent sight of the second dry cove

straight ahead. Follow the well laid path to the foot of Goredale Scar. Having taken a close look at the scar return to the road, turning to the right back over Goredale Bridge and continue along the road for 100 yards and go through the gate on the left signed "Riverside Path to Malham 1½ miles" onto the National Trust's Janet's Foss Malham Estate. Take care as you scramble down the rocks to reach the waterfall of Janet's Foss. From the falls simply follow the clear path which follows the course of Goredale Beck through the deciduous woodland carpeted with wild garlic in the spring. Emerging at the edge of the woodland continue following the path beside the beck, past a field barn and onto a section of flagged path around the edge of the meadows.

Fingerpost to Goredale Scar

Limestone pavement on top of Malham Cove

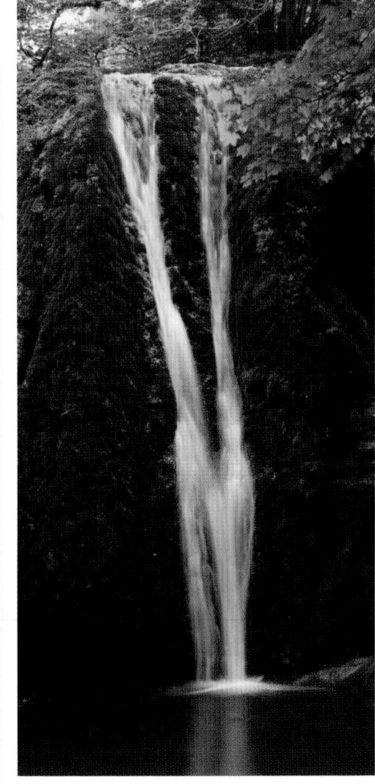
Janet's Foss

Sheep in meadows near Malham

5 Just past Mires Barn a junction of paths is reached, turn right to follow the route of the Pennine Way again back to Malham, signed "FP Malham ¼ mile". With Malham Cove once again in view in the foreground the path makes its way through the fields beside Malham Beck back to Malham. Just past the entrance to the car park cross back over the beck on an ancient footbridge and back to the start.

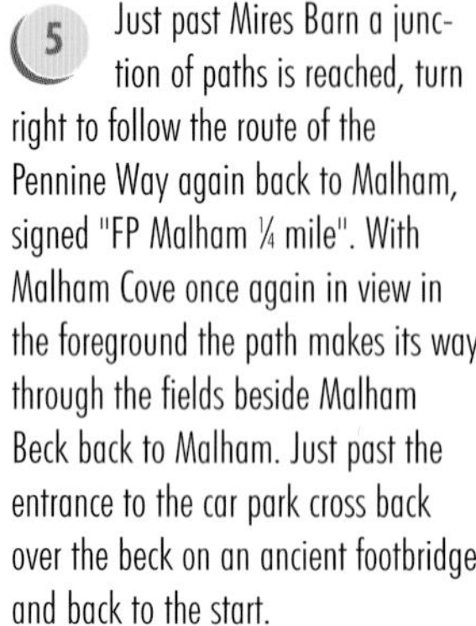

Goredale Scar

2 Malham Tarn and Cove

Take a stroll through the magnificent limestone landscape above Malham Cove

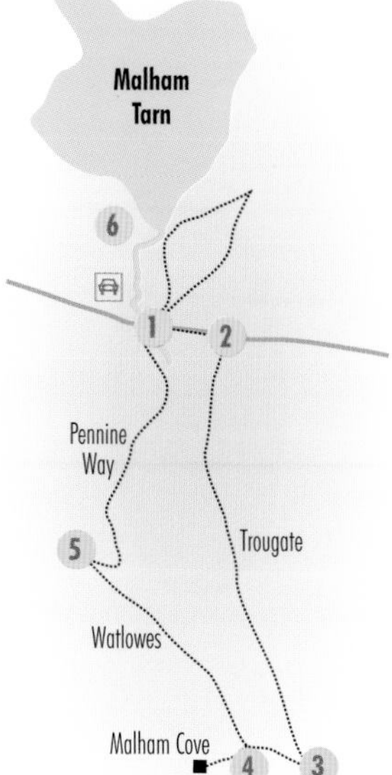

This second route in the Malham area gives the opportunity to further explore the magnificent limestone landscape and dry valleys above Malham Cove. It's almost two walks in one, with the main route being a walk along the two dry valleys south of Malham Tarn, followed by an extension to visit Malham Tarn itself. Watlowes is a spectacular deep side valley, cut by Ice Age melt waters through the limestone. Malham Tarn is also a relic from the Ice Age being damned by glacial moraine, its level being raised by the hand of man in 1791 with the construction of the outlet damn and weir by Lord Ribblesdale.

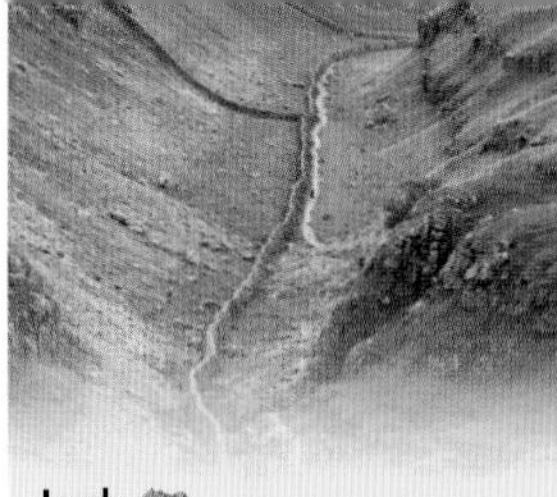

Level:
Length: 3.75 miles (6km)
Ascent: 300 feet (75m)
Terrain: Easy walking on clear paths with one sharp climb up steps
Park and Start: Car park at Malham Tarn on the National Trust's Malham Cove Estate
Info: No facilities on route, but plenty down in Malham itself www.malhamdale.co.uk

Watlowes dry valley

1 Leave the car park and walk east along the road for 400 hundred yards away from the cattle grid near the car park entrance to meet with a path which crosses the road.

2 Turn right to follow the green path across the moor which is signed "FP Malham Raikes 1½ mile". The path gently rises before levelling off. A limestone wall is soon reached, cross over the ladder stile and continue straight on across the short cropped turf path towards a fingerpost which marks a cross roads of paths. Continue straight on signed "FP Malham Cove 1 mile" passing between a series of

Walker on ladder stile approaching Malham Cove

water-logged and mud-filled shake holes. Continue on the path along the dry valley towards Malham Cove with limestone outcrops to either side. Crossing a ladder stile over another drystone wall the path narrows and enters the dry valley of Ewe Moor. Passing through another drystone wall the path gently descends towards the top of Malham Cove. The view opens out to the south and the limestone pavement along the top of Malham Cove comes into sight. The path descends to meet a wall, and over another ladder stile. Follow the "Public Footpath" fingerpost which points directly across the next field to join a path at the next wall.

Heading down to Malham Cove

Approaching the top of Watlowes

3 Turn right to follow the footpath towards Malham Cove barely ¼ mile away. The view of the dry valley overlooked by limestone crags which is the return route is seen straight ahead. The path drops down to pass through a gateway to reach the limestone pavement across the top of Malham Cove.

Limestone pavement above Malham Cove

4 To continue immediately turn right following the sign "Pennine Way" to follow the well worn path up through Watlowes. Pass through one of the gated double wall stiles to re-enter the Ewe Moor Estate. The path passes by a magnificent array of limestone architecture.

Approaching the head of the valley the path narrows and starts to gently rise overlooked by the towering limestone crags. Over a wooden stile at the end of the valley the path steeply rises on stone steps to climb out of the end of the valley.

5 Climb over the double stile at the top and follow the sign to the "Pennine Way FP Malham Tarn 1 mile" along the path which doubles back along the top of the crags. After 150 yards the path swings around to the left to go along a dry limestone side valley. Approaching the end of this valley a drystone wall begins on

Flora in the grikes above Malham Cove

Watlowes dry valley

the right, keep to the path beside the wall. As the valley opens out keep to the wide green path with the wall on the right. Before long the cars at the car park come back into view. Simply follow the wide green path back to the road where it's less than 100 yards back to the start.

The walk follows the route of the Pennine Way from Malham Cove back to the start. The Pennine Way is a 268 mile (429km) long distance National Trail, some 20% of its length is through the Yorkshire Dales National Park.

Malham Tarn

6 To visit Malham Tarn from the car park take the path signed "Pennine Way FP Malham Tarn ¼ mile". The wide green path heads across the moorland with Malham Tarn House in view on the opposite shore of the tarn. Upon reaching the outflow from the tarn the path swings around to the right and proceeds along the southern shore of the tarn with a pair of boathouses on the opposite shore either side of Malham Tarn House. The path passes around the edge of a walled tree plantation. Upon reaching the end of the walled plantation a wide green path doubles back across the moorland to return to the car park.

3 Settle and Attermire Scar

Explore the limestone wonderland above Settle

This walk starts from the busy market town of Settle, start point for the famous Settle to Carlisle Railway line. After a gentle climb above Settle, the walk features more spectacular limestone architecture, this time the impressive limestone crags of Warrendale Knotts and Attermire Scar. The route also gives a chance to visit both Victoria and Jubilee Caves, but take heed of the warnings and Do Not Enter either. Victoria Cave was excavated in 1837 where evidence of brown bear and reindeer from 12,000 years ago just after the last Ice Age was found, even more amazing was evidence of hippopotamus dating as far back as 130,000 years ago.

Jubilee Cave
5
6
Langcliffe
Victoria Cave
Warrendale Knotts
Attermire Scar
4
er Ribble
1
Upper Settle
High Hill
3
2
Mitchell Lane
Lambert Lane (Track)

Level:
Length: 5.5 miles (8.8km)
Ascent: 1000 feet (300m)
Terrain: Steady climb out of Settle along narrow lanes, followed by field paths to the scar and caves
Park and Start: Parking in the Greenfoot car park towards the back of Settle
Info: Toilets and refreshments in Settle

Settle

Sheepfold along Lambert Lane above Settle

1 Leave the car park on the footpath signed "Footpath to The Green and Upper Settle" which rises through the trees at the back of the car park. The path rises past a children's play area and emerges onto a narrow street, turn right to walk towards The Green. At The Green immediately turn left to continue rising past the traditional telephone box, past Lower Croft Street and Greenhead Terrace up Greenhead Lane to arrive at a junction of roads at the top of the town. Turn to the right signed "Pennine Bridleway Long Preston 3½" and also to "The Pinfold 150 yards" along the narrow lane which leaves Upper Settle. Proceed along the narrow single tracked Mitchell Lane. Pass by The Pinfold picnic area and continue straight on along the surfaced lane which starts to gently rise up the hillside. The lane steadily rises heading south east away from Settle with occasional glimpses over the wall back down onto the town. Approaching Blacks Plantation the lane levels off and forks; take the left hand fork signed "Pennine Bridleway Settle Loop" onto the narrow unsurfaced walled Lambert Lane. After barely 100 yards the track forks again and again take the left fork. The ancient Lambert Lane meanders across the hillside between green pastures heading towards High Hill Lane with High Hill the hill beyond.

Walker checks the way along Stockdale Lane

Lime kiln above Stockdale Lane

2 Just past the derelict Preston's Barn Lambert Lane meets up with the surfaced High Hill Lane overlooked by High Hill. Turn right and walk along the road signed "Pennine Bridleway Stockdale Lane". After 50 yards the road forks; take the left fork down Stockdale Lane. Stockdale Lane gently rises beside the slopes of High Hill. Where the lane bends sharply to the right continue straight on over the ladder stile over the wall onto the footpath signed to "Attermire Scar".

3 The path continues to gently rise beside a drystone wall. Arriving at the top of the rise a fine limestone kiln is passed on the left and the view opens out to the impressive limestone scars of Warrendale Knotts. The wide green path continues through the fields heading towards the limestone scars and passing by the distinctively-shaped Sugar Loaf Hill. The path passes through a fence and a fingerpost points the way "Public Footpath" heading towards the cliffs of Attermire Scar to the front right. The path drops down in front of the limestone scars to a system of stone walls. Climb the stile over the drystone wall beneath the scars; to continue head to the right on the green path following the fingerpost signed "Victoria Cave ½ mile".

4 Just past a pile of ancient iron work dated 1860 the path forks, take the left fork which rises to gain access to the dry valley beneath Attermire Scar. The path picks its way through the boulder-strewn valley. Go through the walkers' gate through the wall on the right beneath the scars and continue rising on the well-worn gravel path. The path levels off and the entrance to Victoria Cave comes into view at the front right. Smearsett Scar from Walk 4 can be seen across the Ribble Valley in the distance on the left. Make the detour up to the entrance of Victoria Cave. You are strongly warned not to go into Victoria Cave or near the entrance due to the danger of rock falls. Leaving Victoria Cave behind continue along the path. Passing through a gate the path joins with a clear farm track. To visit Jubilee Cave continue heading straight on along the track for 150 yards where the cave entrance will be seen along a green path just to the right of the track in more exposed limestone.

Warrendale Knotts

Victoria Cave

5 To return to Settle turn left through the gate and follow the farm track which starts to descend the hillside with open views across the Ribble Valley.

6 The track passes over a cattle grid before arriving at the road out of Settle and immediately go through the gate through the wall on the left signed "Bridleway Settle 2 miles", to follow a clear high level path heading back towards Settle. The path passes above the village of Langcliffe in the valley bottom and the

Attermire Scar

Adjacent to the car park entrance stands the "Folly"; a magnificent seventeenth century building which is Grade 1 Listed. Built in 1679 by Richard Preston, a wealthy local merchant, the building features a range of mullion windows which stretches the whole length of the ground floor.

hamlet of Stackhouse on the opposite side of the river. The clear bridleway gradually loses height as it heads along the valley passing through numerous gated walls at the field boundaries. Settle comes into view with the tracks of the Settle to Carlisle railway running along the valley. Continuing to lose height the path passes through a narrow enclosure. Passing by a derelict barn the bridleway enters a narrow walled lane which continues to drop down towards Settle. The lane makes its way through Settle; keep following the bridleway signs through the back of the town. The road emerges at the Market Square; turn left to walk past The Talbot Arms and then straight on back into the car park at the start.

Entrance to Jubilee Cave

Looking along Ribblesdale

4 Stainforth, Feizor and the Ribble

Pass by the spectacular Smearsett Scar on this gentle roller-coaster between valleys

Level: ♥ ♥
Length: 6 miles (9.6km)
Ascent: 1000 feet (300m)
Terrain: Field and riverside paths with a couple of steady climbs
Park and Start: From the YDNP car park in Stainforth just off the B6479 Settle to Horton-in-Ribblesdale road GR820 672
Info: Refreshments from Elaine's Tearooms, Feizor

There are a host of different elements to enjoy on this Ribblesdale walk. First of all the route crosses the line of the Settle to Carlisle Railway, where you may be lucky enough to catch sight of a steam train special in the summer months. Moving on the route crosses Stainforth Bridge over the Ribble just upstream from the rushing waters of Stainforth Force. As height is gained yet another spectacular limestone feature is passed, this time in the form of Smearsett Scar and Pott Scar, before dropping down to pass through the pretty dales hamlet of Feizor with the rather special Elaine's Tearoom. Finally after walking back over the moor the route finishes following the course of the River Ribble upstream along the Ribble Way.

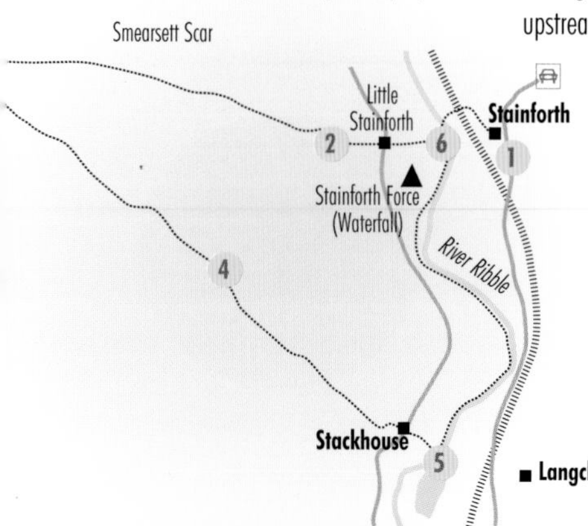

Stainforth Force on the Ribble

1 Leave the car park and cross over the B6479; turn right and walk along the footpath beside the road towards Horton in Ribblesdale. Take the first lane on the left which is marked "Unsuitable for Caravans". The road crosses a bridge over the Settle to Carlisle Railway; follow the lane down the hill to the river. The lane swings around to the left and proceeds beside the Ribble before turning to the right to cross over the river over Stainforth Bridge. Keep to the narrow lane as it rises towards the hamlet of Little Stainforth. After passing the impressive whitewashed hall dated 1724 arrive at the crossroads in the middle of Little Stainforth and go straight across. As the surfaced lane turns into a farmyard continue straight ahead though a gate onto the public footpath which rises up the hillside out of the back of the hamlet.

Smearsett Scar

The Ribble Way is a 72 mile (113km) long distance trail which follows the course of the River Ribble, through the counties of North Yorkshire and Lancashire. Traditionally described running from sea to source, the walk starts at Longton on the Lancashire Coast and follows the river all the way to its source near Horton in Ribblesdale.

2 As the track turns to the left take the path to the front right which continues to rise following the fingerpost signed to Feizor. The path rises up the hillside giving glimpses of the domed summit of Pen-y-ghent along Ribblesdale. At a minor limestone scar the path turns to

the left and continues to gently rise up the hillside on a green path. As the green path flattens out the top of Smearsett Scar comes into view to the front right and the path continues heading towards a wide gate through the wall ahead with an adjacent ladder stile. Continue on the wide green path through the gate with a great view of Pen-y-ghent across the valley to the right. After another slight rise the full length of Smearsett Scar and Potts Scar appear in front; simply follow the short cropped green path along the valley. Cross a drystone wall over a large ladder stile and keep following the green path along the valley signed to Feizor below the limestone outcrops. Over another ladder stile and continue heading straight on. Approaching the end of the valley the view opens out to the north west and the path drops down to the village of Feizor. Keep the wall on your left as you walk through the last field before passing through the back of Scar Close Farm and onto the minor road through Feizor.

Walking towards Feizor

3 Turn left and walk along the lane through Feizor for 100 yards before taking the "Public Bridleway to Scar Top 1⅓ miles and FP Stackhouse 1 mile" up the unsurfaced lane on the left. The path starts to gently rise beside a drystone wall on the left, passing the trees of Bells

Signpost in Feizor

Wood. Keep to the wide green path to the right of the drystone wall as the path continues to gently rise. At the end of the wall keep going straight on up the wide green path and after a couple of hundred yards where the path clearly forks take the left hand path which continues to rise. As the path levels off go through a gate through a wall straight ahead with a retrospective view to the distinctive shape of Ingleborough. The path continues straight on across these high open pastures. The path is joined by a wall on the right. The path passes by sections of exposed limestone on this high level path between Feizor and Stackhouse.

4 Go through a wooden gateway and after barely 20 yards go through the gateway in the wall on the right and continue following the path straight on beside the wall on the left. Passing through another gate the view opens out to reveal a panorama of the Ribble valley. Continue straight on the clear path which starts to descend down to Stackhouse and the river. Approaching a wall above Stackhouse with woods to the front left there are two ladder stiles over the wall. Follow the clearer of the two paths over the ladder stile on the left. Follow the unclear path straight on dropping down towards Stackhouse.

The path drops steeply down the last pasture to join a farm track at a fingerpost above some trees. Turn right at the fingerpost signed "Stackhouse Lane" and follow the track beside the wall into Stackhouse. Keep following the track down to the main road through Stackhouse. Upon reaching the main road go across the road to the front left to follow the "Public Footpath Ribbleway Stainforth 1¼ miles". The narrow walled path heads down to the river.

5 The path joins the riverside path at a weir; turn left and follow the clear path upstream following the Ribble Way back up to Stainforth Bridge. The path passes a disused mill on the opposite bank. Just before reaching Stainforth Bridge the Ribble pours over the impressive triple set of falls that is Stainforth Force.

6 Upon reaching the bridge all that remains is to turn right and walk back up the lane retracing the outbound steps back to the start.

Pen-y-ghent from above Stackhouse

5 Around Austwick Beck

A delightful stroll around Austwick Beck

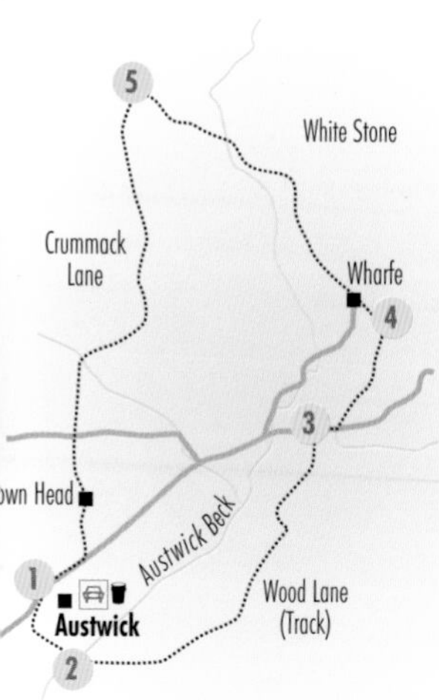

This is a delightful route on the narrow lanes around the Dales village of Austwick; walking doesn't get much easier than this! Initially walking along the ancient Wood Lane to the hamlet of Wharfe, which has nothing whatsoever to do with its more famous namesake, the River Wharfe some 9 miles distant to the north west. The route then climbs following White Stone Lane into Crummackdale, a hanging valley above Austwick, before returning along Crummack Lane back to the start. The route passes two examples of Wash Dubs, used by generations of shepherds to wash their flock prior to shearing.

Level:
Length: 4.25 miles (6.8km)
Ascent: 500 feet (150m)
Terrain: Easy walking on narrow walled lanes throughout
Park and Start: Austwick Village Green (opposite the Game Cock Inn) GR 767 684
Info: Refreshments from the Game Cock Inn- where else?!

White Stones from Crummack Lane

Game Cock Inn, Austwick

1 Start from the village green opposite the Game Cock Inn. From the inn walk 100 yards back to the road junction by the church. At the market cross opposite the church take the road on the left signed to Settle. Cross the bridge over Austwick Beck; note the sheep wash in the wall on the far side of the beck.

2 Immediately over the bridge take the unsurfaced lane on the left signed "Bridleway Feizor 1¾ miles". Walk along the walled Wood Lane with the trees of Oxenber Wood in the foreground. Keep on the lane ignoring the footpath to the right to Feizor. At a junction of walled lanes continue on the lane to the front right along the narrowing Wood Lane. Where the lane next forks, continue along the left hand lane heading towards the hamlet of Wharfe. Upon reaching Wood End Farm keep on the unsurfaced farm track to the left.

Looking along Austwick Beck

Approaching Wharfe

Situated high above Austwick, the Norber Erratic boulders sit on top a limestone pavement. These massive Silurian rocks were scooped up by glaciers in the last Ice Age from the floor of Crummackdale and left high above the valley floor when the ice retreated.

3 Upon reaching the road turn right and walk along the road heading towards Wharfe. Take the unsurfaced lane on the left beside a barn signed "Public Bridleway Wharfe ⅓ mile". Don't worry about the sign "Private Road" – it is a right of way along the "Public Footpath and Bridleway".

4 Continue on the lane through Wharfe bearing left and then take the track up to the right beside Garth Cottage which starts to rise around the back of Wharfe's cottages. The enclosed lane steadily rises and passes a couple of Dales barns. As height is gained there is the occasional glimpse over the wall to the south west. The lane narrows and levels off and proceeds at this higher level above the unseen Austwick Beck. Look

Field barn above Austwick

Vertical rock strata

out for the vertical folded rock strata on the hill over the wall on the left. The narrow lane passes by a third barn. Rowan trees grow either side of the lane and are festooned with red berries in late summer. Approaching the top of the route the lane crosses the beck using one of the two clapper gate bridges adjacent to the wash dub field. Having crossed the stream keep following the lane on the opposite bank towards the limestone-scarred hill on the horizon.

5 At a T junction with another lane turn left to head back down Crummack Lane all the way down back to Austwick. The unsurfaced Crummack Lane heads down the valley with outstanding views of the Western Dales scenery in all directions. Pass the entrance to Sowerthwaite Farm where the lane is surfaced and the road continues to descend with open views to the south west. Simply keep to the lane as it drops down to pass a small wood and continues all the way down into Austwick. The lane passes through Austwick Town Head and arrives at the main road and all that remains is to turn right to walk back into the centre of the village passing by the school on the way back to the start.

Crossing Austwick Beck over the ancient clapper bridge

6 Clapham Beck and Trow Gill

A chance to visit Ingleborough Cave on the way back from Trow Gill

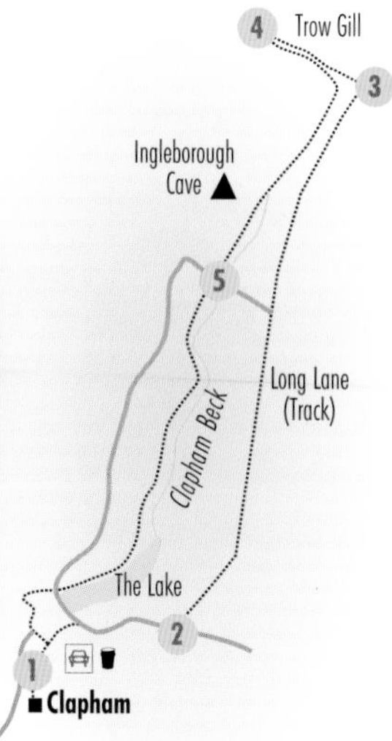

This super little walk around Clapham Beck fully explores all the delights that Clapham has to offer. Starting from the centre of the village the route passes by Clapham's elaborate Millennium Stone which celebrates a thousand years of local history, before heading upstream on Long Lane high above the beck. At the head of the valley, Trow Gill, yet another spectacular dry limestone ravine is visited. Returning along Clapdale Drive, you can take the opportunity to visit the underground labyrinth of the famous Ingleborough Cave. Finally the route passes through the Ingleborough Estate Nature Trail with its grotto, lake and fine display of rhododendrons brought from the Far East by Reginald Farrer.

Level:
Length: 4.25 miles (6.8km)
Ascent: 750 feet (225m)
Terrain: Easy walking on lanes and clear paths with gentle climb onto Long Lane
Park and Start: YDNP car park in Clapham (GR 745 692)
Info: Refreshments and toilets at the start. www.ingleboroughcave.co.uk Small fee to pay to pass through the Ingleborough Estate Nature Trail

Tree-lined lane past Encomb Bridges

1 Leave the car park and turn right to walk further up the village. Pass the gated entrance to Ingleborough Hall. Approaching the top of the village and just before the church of St James take the unsurfaced lane up to the right signed "BW Austwick" passing by the Clapham 2000 millennium stone and around the back of the church. The lane gently rises passing through a pair of long dark tunnels which are the Encomb Bridges. The stony walled lane now steadily rises passing between deciduous woodland to either side.

Walking along Long Lane

Disused gateposts along Long Lane

2 The track levels off and then forks; take the left hand fork beside the wood with Thwaite and Norber Scars to the font left signed "BW Selside 4¾". The lane drops down beside the wood before bending to the left and beginning to rise again. Reaching the top of the rise with Thwaite Scars to the front right, Long Lane levels off and continues heading in a northerly direction. Walking along Clapdale with views across to the left to Clapdale Farm and Barn, the track passes through a gate and the entrance to Ingleborough Cave can be seen in the valley bottom down on the left.

Looking down onto the entrance to Ingleborough Cave

3 Beneath Thwaite Scars and just before the track bends and starts to rise, a ladder stile is seen on the left over a wall with another ladder stile at the bottom of the field. Climb the ladder stile to drop steeply down the stony meadow, and climb over the ladder stile at the bottom to reach the main path which runs along the valley. To immediately return to Clapham turn left but it is far better to turn right to take the detour to look at the steep confines of Trow Gill. The path gently rises and passes through a gate to enter the drystone valley of Trow Gill. Continue up the sheer sided Trow Gill to the cave at the top of the dry valley just before the path rises to climb steeply out of the top of the valley. This is the most suitable point to turn around to commence the return to Clapham.

The Farrer family were lords of the manor for over 200 years, and much of Clapham as seen today was planned and built in the 1830s by the family, including Ingleborough Hall. The nature trail commemorates Reginald Farrer a renowned botanist and plant collector.

Leave Long Lane here!

4 Simply head back along the path back down Trow Gill and then continue along the valley path to the entrance to Ingleborough Cave. The path passes over a packhorse bridge over Clapham Beck at the entrance to Ingleborough Cavern, renowned as being one of the best show caves in England. Continue heading back towards Clapham on the dressed track beside Clapham Beck.

5 The path enters the wooded Ingleborough Estate Trail through a metal gate for which there is a small fee to pay at the exit. It's a delightful stroll along the Ingleborough Trail beside the tree-lined Clapham Beck. The path passes by a building known as The Grotto. Approaching Clapham the path passes by the imaginatively named "The Lake". At the end of the lake take the track to the left signed "Way Out". Leave the estate and walk back through the village passing the falls in Clapham Beck on the left. Cross the bridge over the beck and walk past the church to head back to the start.

Sheep in cave at top of Trow Gill

"The Lake"

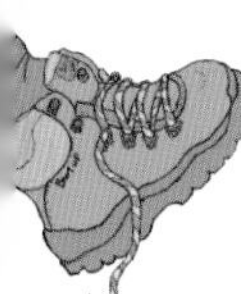

7 Ingleton Waterfalls

Enjoy the magnificent falls along the twin rivers Twiss and Doe

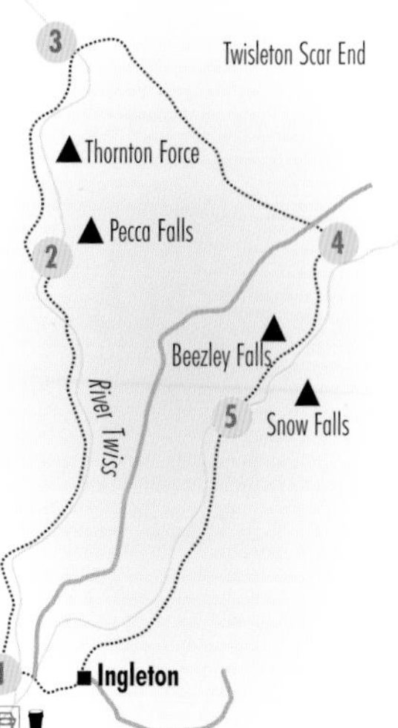

The Ingleton Waterfalls Trail is one of the most popular walks in the Yorkshire Dales and so more than justifies its place in this collection of "leisure walks in the Western Dales.

Initially following the course of the River Twiss passing the multi-tiered Pecca Falls, the trail reaches the impressive Thornton Force beneath Twisleton Scars. The upper reaches of the return leg are even more spectacular than the outbound route passing by Beezley, Rival and Snow Falls. You are strongly advised to follow the safety instructions at the start of the trail and to keep to the well laid footpaths; in particular there are some sections on the return leg where small children will need to be held tightly by the hand.

Level:
Length: 4.25 miles (7km)
Ascent: 600 feet (180m)
Terrain: Well maintained path throughout
Park and Start: Ingleton Waterfalls Trail car park GR693 733
Info: Toilets and refreshments at start. There is a charge to enter the trail, for latest pricing log on to www.ingletonwaterfallstrail.co.uk

1 Leave through the back of the car park heading upstream already with the sound of the River Twiss on the right. The well maintained path proceeds beside the tree-lined River Twiss where there is plenty of evidence of coppicing activities within the hazel wood. The path climbs over a gorge on concrete steps and then passes through a deep ravine with high cliffs to either side. The route then follows the course of the river upstream gradually gaining height all the while. Cross the Twiss over Manor Bridge, an iron footbridge. The path now makes its way up the eastern bank of the river heading towards the first Pecca Falls. The first Pecca Falls viewing area provides an ideal place to stop, before the path continues on past this point.

River Twiss near the start

2 Follow the route back across the Twiss over Pecca Bridge with the impressive set of Pecca Falls just upstream. The path rises to pass beside the multi-stepped falls of Pecca Falls – four main drops – and then continues to rise passing Holly Bush Spout just beyond Pecca Falls and

passes by a seasonal refreshment hut. Approaching the top of Thornton Dale the trees thin and the view opens out to open fellside and finally the magnificent spectacle of Thornton Force comes into view. The path now climbs up a flight of steps out of the dale beside Thornton Force. Above Thornton Force the view opens out still further to the head of the dale with the exposed limestone of Twisleton Scar on the horizon. Keep following the path round with the river flowing down on the right. Swing around to the left with a view along the limestone-faced Kingsdale.

The trail has been open since 1885. Much of the trail has been designated as a Site of Special Scientific Interest (SSSI) in recognition of its rare plants and geological features. 500 million years of geological history can be traced through the rocks along the trail.

Pecca Falls

Thornton Force

Crossing the bridge at the top of the walk

Ingleborough from the top of the trail

3 Cross the Twiss for one last time over the footbridge at the head of the dale and continue on the path as it rises up the opposite bank. The path emerges through a gate to arrive at an unsurfaced walled lane; turn right to walk along the lane heading towards the River Doe in the adjacent valley. From the lane there are wide open vistas to the south and west. The lane passes beneath the limestone Twisleton Scar and around the back of Twisleton Hall. Continue straight on following the signs for the Waterfalls Walk heading towards Beezley Falls. The huge dome of Ingleborough comes into view. With the River Doe in sight the path joins a single track road opposite the modern quarry; follow the signs to go straight on down the road to pass by the Falls Refreshment Centre, heading towards Beezley Falls.

Rival Falls

Beezley Falls

4 Head down into the trees to immediately arrive at the noisy Beezley Falls. Rival Falls are shortly arrived at; the path hugs the river bank as it steeply descends the dale. The path makes its way to Baxenghyll Gorge: do not miss the opportunity to walk down the viewing bridge to be able to appreciate this spectacular, narrow and deep walled gorge. Finally Snow Falls are passed with views through the trees.

5 The path follows the rushing waters downstream, crosses a narrow footbridge onto the opposite bank below Snow Falls and continues all the way back into Ingleton. The trees thin out as a long abandoned quarry is passed. The path passes by the edge of the modern Ingleton Quarry. With Ingleton in sight the gorge opens out and passes through an array of old quarry workings before finally re-entering the trees for the final stretch into Ingleton. The path widens out onto a surfaced road at the top of the village, just follow it down. Follow the signs through Ingleton back to the Waterfalls Trail car park.

Baxenghyll Gorge

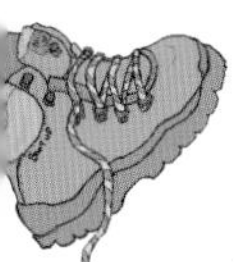

8 Chapel-le-Dale and Twisleton Scars

An exploration of the limestone pavement above Twisleton Scars

This is a tremendous walk combining the best of geological features with some historical interest. Twisleton boasts one of the largest areas of limestone pavement in the country and this walk allows ample opportunity to explore all that it has to offer; vast expanses of clints and grikes, rare and delicate botany, the occasional erratic boulder left from the last Ice Age and sink holes galore.

The bulk of Ingleborough is in view for almost the entire route on the opposite side of the valley. Historical interest is provided by the Ribblehead Viaduct and St Leonard's church burial place for some of the workers on the viaduct. The route returns to Chapel-le-Dale along the Roman Road which runs all the way from Ingleton to Bainbridge in Wensleydale.

2 Ellerdale
Chapel-le-Dale
1
3
Twisleton
Twisleton Scars
Twisleton Scar End
River Doe
B6255
5

Level: 🥾🥾
Length: 6.75 miles (10.8km)
Ascent: 650 feet (200m)
Terrain: Gentle climb and descent at either end of Twisleton Scars, otherwise easy walking on the level
Park and Start: Chapel-le-Dale church car park just off the B6255
Info: No facilities on route

Walled lane at the end of the ridge

St Leonard's, Chapel-le-Dale

1 Leave the little car park and turn left to walk over the bridge over the young Chapel Beck. Pass by St Leonard's church on the right and immediately past the church take the narrow walled lane up to the right. The single track lane rises leaving Chapel-le-Dale behind. The road forks as it loses its surface, take the right hand fork which goes straight on and continues to rise through woodland signed "BW Ellerbeck 1 mile". The lane meanders its way up the hillside. A sculpture of an archer is passed on the left as the lane continues to steadily gain height. The lonely buildings of Ghyll Head are passed and the view opens out to the slopes of Whernside to the front right. The first outcrops of limestone pavement are passed on either side of the open moorland approaching the isolated hamlet of Ellerbeck and the views expand in both directions with Ingleborough to the front left and a clear view of the impressive Ribblehead Viaduct to the right.

Limestone pavement above Chapel-le-Dale

Ingleborough from the bridleway

2 As the lane reaches the ford over Ellerbeck Gill turn left signed "Bridleway Scar End 3½", to start to cross the moorland on a farm track. After 20 yards the path forks adjacent to two derelict railway wagons. Take the lower left hand fork where a faint path leads its way across the moorland, passes a couple of shakeholes and continues on its way heading south west. The path becomes clearer as it proceeds heading along the valley with extensive views across the dale to the mass of Ingleborough. The bridleway makes its way over the moorland between sections of limestone pavement above Twisleton Scars.

3 The bridleway narrows as it picks its way through an area of limestone pavement in line with the summit of Ingleborough and swings to the left as the green path becomes clearer on the ground again. The vast expanse of limestone pavement which marks the top of Twisleton Scars is passed on the left with the occasional erratic boulder left behind from the end of the last Ice Age. After nearly 3 miles walking along the level the path cuts through a final section of limestone; Morecambe Bay comes into view along with the limestone-scarred face of Keld Head Scar in the next valley to the right. The path passes three stone structures up on the left: two

cairns and a three-sided wind shelter. The route starts to descend on the path cut through the limestone pavement with wide open views to the west out to Morecambe Bay. Where the path forks take the clearer green track on the left. A little further on, with a distinctive drystone wall on the left approaching the end of Twisleton Scars, the path forks again and this time take the right hand fork; this initially feels to be heading in the wrong direction but stick with it because this gives the easier descent down the end of the scar. The path swings around still further to the right heading towards the next valley of Kingsdale where the top of the Ingleton Waterfalls Walk (Walk 7) comes into view.

Erratic on limestone pavement looking towards Ingleborough

The 24 arches of the Ribblehead Viaduct were completed in 1874 and carry trains on the famous Settle to Carlisle railway line. Spanning some 440 yards (400m) it is overlooked to the north by Whernside one of the Yorkshire Three Peaks.

4 The path descends to meet up with a dales lane. Just above a ladder stile the path goes around a hairpin bend back to the left and continues to descend at a gentle angle meeting up with the clear track. Turn left and continue around the base of Twisleton Scar. The lane makes its way around the back of Twisleton Hall. Keep straight on signed "Public Footpath" around the back of the farm buildings, following for a short while the route of the Ingleton Waterfalls Walk, and Ingleborough comes back into sight. The clear path drops down to meet Oddie's Lane with the entrance to White Scar Caves in view on the opposite side of the valley.

Shake hole above Twisleton Scars

5 The path joins the surfaced Oddie's Lane, turn left and follow in the steps of the Romans along the ancient Roman Road all the way back to Chapel-le-Dale. Alternatively make the short detour to the Falls Refreshment Centre before continuing back along Oddie's Lane. There are outstanding views to Ingleborough across the valley all the way back. The road makes its way up the valley with the limestone Twisleton Scars above on the left and the River Doe in the valley bottom. After an easy walk along the valley the road arrives back at Chapel-le-Dale.

The three cairns looking towards Ingleborough

9 Ingleborough

Climb to the top of Yorkshire's second highest hill

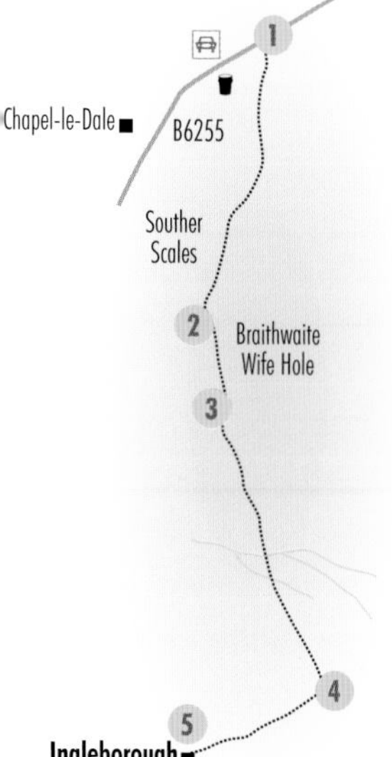

Ingleborough is Yorkshire's second highest peak at 2372 feet (723m) and is the middle of the Three Peaks, with Whernside (the highest and known as "the roof of Yorkshire" at 2415 feet-736m) just to the north and Pen-y-ghent at 2277 feet (694m) to the east. I pondered long and hard about including an ascent to the summit of Ingleborough within this collection of "leisure walks" but eventually concluded that it had to be included given that its distinctive shape is observed from many of the other walks within the collection. I have chosen the most popular and easiest route on clear and well maintained paths (and also the route which involves least climbing)! Save this one for a clear day; the views from the top are extensive to all the surrounding hills extending as far as the Lake District Fells.

Level:

Length: 5 miles (8km)

Ascent: 1400 feet (425m)

Terrain: Steady climb on flagged and stepped path with one very steep section

Park and Start: Road side parking on B6255 above The Old Hill Inn

Info: Refreshments from The Old Hill Inn

Twisleton Scars from Souther Scales

Lamb on Souther Scales

1 Driving away from Ingleton there's plenty of off road parking on the left just past the Old Hill Inn beyond Chapel-le-Dale. Walk back down the road 50 yards to pass by the stone built hut of Chapel-le-Dale Water Treatment Works and immediately go through the gate on the left signed "BW Great Douk FP Ingleborough 2⅜ miles". Walk along the wide unsurfaced track which heads towards the unmistakeable shape of Ingleborough. The track passes by an impressive and well preserved lime-stone kiln on the left. Go through the farm gate through a drystone wall into the next field where the green path goes straight on, these initial sections being on the level. Approaching the end of the second field keep straight on aiming for the metal gate through the wall, don't be tempted to swing up to the left towards a clearer path. Through the metal gate, follow the fingerpost straight on "FP Ingleborough 2 miles". Keeping on the level following the path which goes straight across the third enclosure to a pair of wooden gates. Continue on the wide green path through Souther Scale Nature Reserve with fine views to Twisleton Scars on the opposite side of the valley (Walk 8).

Whernside from Souther Scales

Flagged path to Ingleborough

2 The path rises and swings to the left to emerge beside an impressive section of limestone pavement; keep following the clear track. Keep to the path to avoid damaging any of the limestone pavement on this popular route. The clear track meanders through the area of limestone with the bulk of Ingleborough straight ahead. Just before reaching the intake wall and the open moor, the track passes an enormous hole – Braithwaite Wife Hole.

3 The track passes through one of the double gates through the wall to arrive at the flagged section of pathway where the climb up Ingleborough commences in earnest. Looking over your left shoulder Ribblehead Viaduct can be seen in the distance overlooked by Whernside. The path levels off for a short while as it passes over wooden boardwalk sections as it crosses a peaty bog and then back onto stone flags and steps as the path continues its ascent. As height is gained the views continue to improve with the bulk of Ingleborough dominating the foreground. The path levels off for a while and crosses a couple of culverts with streams running along the bottom of each before continuing the steady climb again on the flagged path across the moorland. The path levels one last time before entering the shadows beneath the seemingly vertical cliff ahead. However a well laid stepped path steeply zig zags up the 300 feet to reach the ridgeback of Ingleborough.

Braithwaite Wife Hole

4 The path emerges through a gate onto Ingleborough's ridge; pause to catch your breath and to enjoy the views. On a clear day the Lakeland Fells are in sight, the Howgills are over Whernside and below Ribblehead Viaduct and following the line of the Settle to Carlisle the summit of Great Knoutberry at the head of Dentdale can be seen (Walk 10). Whilst the steepest climbing is over there is still some way to reach the true summit; continue rising on the pitched path heading to the right towards Ingleborough's summit. All of a sudden the path emerges onto the gritstone summit plateau of Ingleborough. To reach the true summit pass by several cairns on the northerly edge and continue to gently rise to reach the well-built four-armed wind shelter and the now redundant OS column. The true summit is the untidy mound furthest to the west. Take your time to walk around the north-western edge of the summit plateau with outstanding views across to Twisleton Scars, the Lake District Fells and the Howgills.

O.S. column with summit cairn in the background

Approaching the summit

5 Whilst there are many paths on Ingleborough the simplest way to return is to retrace the outbound route on the well prepared path all the way back down to the start enjoying the extensive views along the way.

Situated on top of Ingleborough's summit plateau are the remains of an Iron Age Fort. Faint traces of the walls can be observed around the rim of the summit. Despite having survived 1,000 years it is the ravages of the last 20 that have done the worst damage! Stones from the fort have been displaced by the army of modern day cairn builders- please leave everything as you find it!

Path to the summit plateau

Summit wind shelter

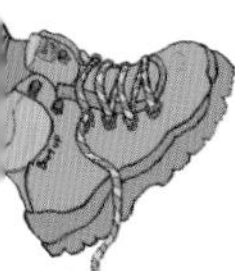

10 Head of Dentdale

Enjoy full length views along Dentdale and a fine railway viaduct at close quarters

Dentdale, the most northerly of the Western Dales, is generally accessed from the Cumbrian market town of Sedburgh, its relative inaccessibility adding to its charms. The village of Dent lies roughly half way along the dale and it is from Dent Station that the walk starts. However Dent Station, England's highest main line railway station on the Settle to Carlisle Railway, is actually some 4 miles further along the dale at the head of the valley. The walk makes its way around the flanks of Great Knoutberry Hill guarding the head of the dale and offers full length views along the valley. The route passes beneath the spectacular Arten Gill Viaduct which carries the railway high above the valley floor.

2
1 Dent Station
Settle Carlisle Railway
5
Cow Dub
3
4
Arten Gill
Artengill Viaduct

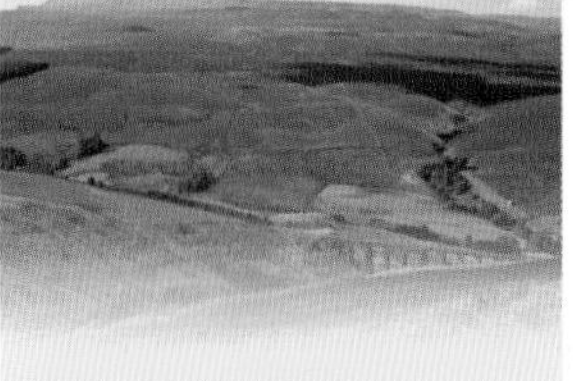

Level: ♥ ♥ ♥
Length: 6 miles (9.6km)
Ascent: 1200 feet (360m)
Terrain: Roads and bridleways throughout with stiff climb to begin and end with
Park and Start: Dent Railway Station (GR 763 875)
Info: Refreshments from The Sportsman's Inn at Cow Dub

Farmer turning hay in the valley bottom

Dent Railway Station

1 Park in the station yard, leave the station yard and turn right immediately rising to cross the bridge over the railway line. Simply follow the single track road which steadily rises up the hillside along the road heading towards Garsdale. After about half a mile of steady ascent the unmistakeable shape of Ingleborough appears on the horizon to the right together with the whaleback ridge of Whernside. The cairns which line Pikes Edge on the slopes of Great Knoutberry Hill are clearly seen on the right. A pine plantation on the left is left behind as the road continues to steadily climb.

2 Approaching the top of the road a very clear unsurfaced lane joins from the right and this is the way forward for the high level route around the head of Dentdale; go through the gate signed "Bridleway Only". The once walled lane continues to rise for a short while before levelling off as it proceeds around the slopes of Great Knoutberry Hill with extensive views along Dentdale with

Artengill Viaduct

Whernside, Great Coum and Aye Gill Pike all in view. The track passes through an iron kissing gate overlooked by the cairns on the horizon with the twin peaks of Ingleborough and Whernside in clear view in the foreground. The track passes over the top of Harber Gill, below there are rows of vertically placed railway sleepers above the railway line to keep the worst of the snow from the winter gales off the track. In line with Whernside and passing through a wooden five bar gate, the upland track now starts to swing around to the left heading east. The lane crosses the ford over Brant Nook where there are fine views looking down into Arten Gill with the walled lane which is the next stage of the route clearly in view along the valley bottom.

3 Approaching the head of the dale the lane swings around to the right and starts to descend to a sheepfold at the head of Arten Gill where the lane turns to the right for the long steady descent down to the valley. Even on a relatively still day the wind is funnelled up Arten Gill. The walled lane steadily descends following Arten Gill down to the impressive Artengill Viaduct. The track passes beneath the high stone arches of Artengill Viaduct and continues on its way losing height to the valley bottom. The track emerges onto the road at the pretty dales hamlet of Carlow Hill; continue straight on along the road through the hamlet.

Artengill Viaduct is constructed from the impressively named Dent Marble. However Dent Marble is actually a dark form of limestone with a high fossil content. Quarried locally it became popular for fire surrounds and balustrades.

Cow Dub

4 At the bottom of the village cross the very narrow pack-horse bridge over the river and join the main valley road as it swings to the right following the route of the Dales Way long distance trail footpath along the road heading towards Cowgill. Take the normal precautions when walking along this quiet valley road, listening out for any approaching vehicles and keeping to the right side of the road. The road proceeds adjacent to the young River Dee. The road passes through the hamlet of Cow Dub with the whitewashed Sportsman's Inn.

Dentdale from slopes of Great Knoutberry Hill

5 Eventually the road crosses the river over Lea Yeat Bridge. Prepare yourself for the sting in the tail; namely the ascent up the single track road, back up to Dent Station three quarters of a mile away. Simply follow the road as it steeply rises back up to the station pausing to enjoy the great views along Dentdale from the road on the climb.

Packhorse bridge over the River Dee

Dentdale from the road back up to the station